Cornerstones of Freedom

The USS Arizona

R. Conrad Stein

CP CHILDRENS PRESS®

CHICAGO

Library of Congress Cataloging-in-Publication Data

Stein, R. Conrad.
  The USS Arizona / by R. Conrad Stein.

    p. cm. — (Cornerstones of freedom)
  Summary: Discusses the 1941 Japanese attack on Pearl
Harbor, with an emphasis on the fate of the USS
Arizona.
  ISBN 0-516-06656-0
  1. USS Arizona (Ship)—Juvenile literature. 2. Pearl
Harbor (Hawaii), Attack on, 1941—Juvenile literature.
[1. USS Arizona (Ship) 2. Pearl Harbor (Hawaii),
Attack on, 1941.] I. Title. II. Series
D767.92.S834 1992   91-44646
940.54'26—dc20   CIP
                                           AC

Most of the men on board the USS *Arizona* were asleep below decks. It was Sunday, and the huge battleship was docked at Pearl Harbor in the Hawaiian Islands. The few men on watch looked at the rising sun and felt the warm Pacific breezes. Tony Muncie, an eighteen-year-old crewman, told himself that it would be a beautiful day—the kind of day that brings tourists flocking to Hawaii. The young sailor had no idea that this day, December 7, 1941, would become a day that shocked the world.

Thousands of miles away, at a Japanese naval base, Admiral Isoroku Yamamoto nervously

All was peaceful when these U.S. bombers flew in formation over Hawaii a few days before the Japanese attack on Pearl Harbor.

Japanese planes prepare to take off for the raid on Pearl Harbor.

checked his watch. He calculated what the time was in Hawaii and nodded to himself. More than two hundred Japanese airplanes were now winging their way toward Pearl Harbor. The planes had taken off from aircraft carriers. They were on their way to destroy the United States Pacific Fleet. Yamamoto, Japan's highest-ranking admiral, had planned the entire operation.

Admiral Yamamoto was an intelligent man. As a representative of the Japanese Navy, he had once lived in Washington, D.C. and had come to know many American generals and admirals. Yamamoto loved to gamble and had a reputation in the American capital as an excellent poker player.

Left: Admiral Isoroku Yamamoto Right: A Japanese drawing showing the position of U.S. ships in Pearl Harbor

Now he paced the floor, waiting for the first bombs to be dropped on a nation he admired. Yamamoto did not want this war. He knew that America could build huge fleets of ships and planes and would soon overpower Japan. But the Japanese government was controlled by a group of war lords who argued that their islands were overcrowded and lacked natural resources. Japan needed steel, oil, rubber, and farmland. The war lords insisted that Japan must expand and take over China, Indonesia, and the Philippines to gain the resources of those countries. But the Philippines was a colony of the United States, and China was a United States ally. The United States, with a powerful fleet based in Hawaii, prevented Japanese expansion. The war lords demanded that the fleet be destroyed.

Yamamoto pleaded for peace, but his pleas were ignored. Realizing that war was inevitable, he planned the first battle of a war he believed his country would lose.

There would be no declaration of war. Instead Yamamoto ordered one swift surprise attack designed to destroy the United States fleet. Six of Japan's finest aircraft carriers were sent steaming toward Hawaii. The carriers were protected by two battleships and a dozen cruisers and destroyers. Yamamoto, the poker player, was playing with his highest cards.

Tony Muncie had been in the United States Navy for just six months. The *Arizona* was his first ship, and he was proud of her. He played guard on the ship's basketball team and looked forward to the upcoming game against the team from the battleship *Tennessee*. It was peacetime, and there was little to think about except basketball games and the girls in Honolulu.

Even so, the winds of war blew hot over the Pacific that autumn. Tony noticed the deadly seriousness his shipmates displayed while practicing gunnery with the *Arizona*'s powerful fourteen-inch guns. The older sailors believed that war would come any day. But no one dreamed that the Japanese would strike first at Hawaii. Their ships could not carry enough fuel to cruise to Hawaii and back, and no large striking force could sail those thousands of miles

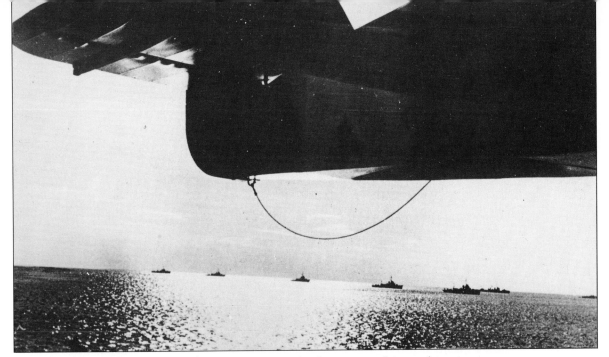

Japanese destroyers patrolled the South China Sea a few weeks before the attack on Pearl Harbor.

without being seen and reported by some ship or airplane. No, Tony thought, if war comes, the Japanese will probably hit the Philippines first.

But Tony and his shipmates did not foresee Yamamoto's brilliant strategy. For months before the attack, his sailors had practiced refueling at sea. Then Yamamoto sent his ships along a course in the Northern Pacific where few ships sailed because of constant storms during the winter. Yamamoto's strategy had worked, and the Japanese fleet now lay unseen two hundred miles off Hawaii while airplanes loaded with bombs and torpedoes sped toward Pearl Harbor.

Tony was on fire watch that morning. It was a routine, peacetime task. If a fire broke out on deck, Tony was to sound the alarm and help the

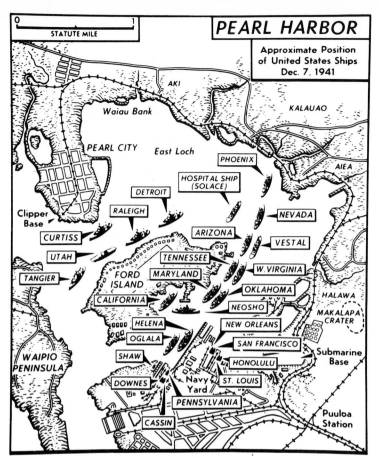

A map showing the position of U.S. ships in Pearl Harbor on December 7, 1941

fire fighters. There was little danger of fire, so Tony walked to the bow of the ship. The *Arizona* was docked just a few feet from the beach off Ford Island—in the middle of Pearl Harbor. She was one of seven giant battleships tied up there, some two by two, others alone.

Tony could name each one of them without having to read the numbers on the sides of the ships. He saw the *Nevada*, the *Tennessee*, the *West Virginia*, the *Maryland*, the *Oklahoma*, and the *California*. Here was the heart of the United States Pacific Fleet. The sailors called this line of ships "Battleship Row."

Tony placed his elbows on the rails of the ship and leaned over the side. The ships in Battleship Row were painted a somber gray. Their giant guns, looming out of turrets, looked like the horns of fierce beasts. Even so, the powerful ships somehow looked peaceful in the morning sunlight, and Tony thought about writing a letter home.

Near Pearl Harbor, a radar station manned by two army privates showed some confusing blips. Minutes later, the screen was covered with dots showing that more than fifty planes were flying toward Pearl Harbor. The excited privates called the duty officer.

"Don't worry about it," the officer said, "those are our own planes."

A flight of American B-17 bombers was expected to arrive from California early that Sunday. The officer assumed that the blips on the radar screen were American planes.

Tony Muncie heard the distant buzzing of airplanes, but he did not look up. He figured it was U.S. Army Air Force planes on maneuvers. Since war tensions were so great, training flights on Sunday were not unusual. Tony wondered if war would come. Perhaps not. Just yesterday, President Roosevelt and Secretary of State Cordell Hull had spoken to two Japanese ambassadors in Washington, D.C. Perhaps the talks would settle the differences between the two countries and there would be no war.

Japanese ambassador Kichisaburo Nomura

The sound of airplane engines grew louder. Suddenly, an explosion thundered with so much power it seemed as if the earth shook. A black cloud of smoke billowed from Ford Island.

At first Tony thought it was just the army practicing bombing, but why would they do this so close to the ships? Then he looked up. The air was filled with planes buzzing about Battleship Row like angry bees. Tony saw flaming red suns painted on the sides of the planes.

"My God," he said, "it's the Japanese."

Others were not so quick to recognize that they were under attack. Aboard the USS *Nevada*, a band and a marine guard stood at attention

Ford Island as seen from a Japanese plane during the attack

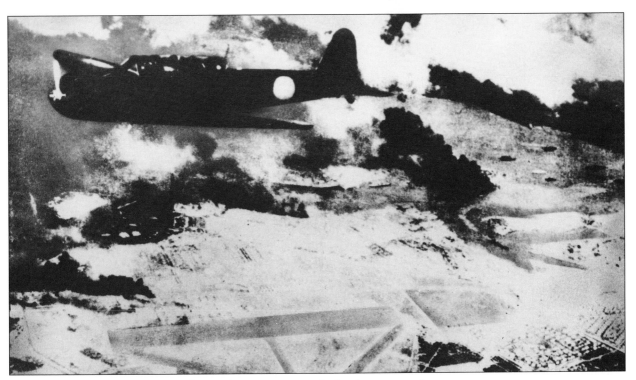

A Japanese bomber makes a run over the harbor as smoke billows from American ships below.

ready to play "The Star-Spangled Banner" and hoist the colors as they did every Sunday morning just before eight o'clock. Halfway through the playing of the national anthem, the rear gunner of a passing Japanese plane sprayed the ship with machine-gun bullets. He hit no one, but his bullets ripped into the flag. The band stopped for a moment. Then years of discipline took hold and the men continued playing. The marine guard stood at rigid attention, and no one broke ranks. At the conclusion of the anthem, the band leader ordered, "Dismissed," and everyone scrambled for cover.

A line of torpedo planes closed in on the

A direct torpedo hit, indicated by ripples in the water, is scored on one of the ships in Battleship Row.

battleship *Oklahoma*. No one was manning the antiaircraft guns, so the planes flew low and sped directly toward their target. Torpedoes dropped from the planes. They splashed into the water and darted toward the battleship, where many of the crew members still slept in cots below decks.

Three torpedoes tore into the *Oklahoma*, and the explosions jarred all of Battleship Row.

Sirens on the other ships screamed. Excited voices shouted over loudspeakers: "We are under attack! This is no drill. Repeat. This is no drill."

Sailors poured onto the decks of the battleships. Some were still in their underwear as they rushed to the antiaircraft guns. But ammunition for the guns was locked in steel compartments. With no one to shoot back at them, Japanese pilots flew so low that American sailors could see their faces. One frustrated sailor threw a monkey wrench at a dive bomber.

The *Tennessee* and the *West Virginia* were tied up side by side along the shore of Ford Island. The *West Virginia* was on the outboard side and took five hits from torpedoes. The *Tennessee* was in between the *West Virginia* and the shore, so no torpedo could hit her; but two armor-piercing bombs from low-flying Japanese planes crashed through her decks and exploded inside the ship.

A navy launch rescues a sailor from the blazing West Virginia.

Three minutes after the first bomb fell on Ford Island, a message that no American would ever forget was radioed to the U.S. mainland:

AIR RAID, PEARL HARBOR—THIS IS NO DRILL.

On the deck of the *Arizona*, Tony Muncie worked furiously passing ammunition to an antiaircraft gun crew. Someone had broken the padlock of an ammunition compartment, and many crew members were now at their battle stations. Finally, Tony thought, we'll be able to fight back.

Before the antiaircraft gun could start to fire, however, a line of Japanese bombers roared over

Small puffs of smoke from American antiaircraft guns dot the sky as a huge black cloud rises from the burning USS Arizona.

The Arizona *exploded after Japanese bombs touched off more than a million pounds of gunpowder stored on the ship.*

the *Arizona* and released their bombs. Five
bombs crashed through the decks of the ship.
One of them exploded below decks in an area
where the powder for the *Arizona*'s huge guns
was stored. There was a thundering explosion.
The *Arizona* erupted into an orange ball of flame.
In that instant, more than eleven hundred men
died. Men on neighboring ships saw the giant
battleship jump halfway out of the water, then
sink like a rock into the mud and shallow water
off Ford Island. Only her upper decks, swept with
flames, poked out of the water.

The USS Maryland *(left) and the capsized USS* Oklahoma *(right)*

Other ships on Battleship Row took quick hits from bombs and torpedoes. Two bombs crashed into the *Maryland.* Torpedoes ripped open the bottom of the *California,* and she began sinking in the shallow water. Smoke billowed from the *Nevada* after bomb hits. Cruisers and destroyers in the harbor were bombed and machine-gunned. Japanese planes even attacked the ancient battleship *Utah,* which was docked away from Battleship Row and was used only for target practice.

Other Japanese planes hit airfields and army bases near Pearl Harbor. At Hickam Field, Japanese planes found dozens of American aircraft parked side by side like cars in a parking lot. In minutes, Japanese machine-gun fire made flaming wrecks of the American planes. A 550-pound bomb crashed through the roof of a barracks at Hickam and exploded in the dining hall—where hundreds of men were eating breakfast.

As the bombing continued, American forces recovered from the shock of the surprise attack and began fighting back. At the airfields, men pushed undamaged fighter planes away from those that were blazing nearby. The undamaged planes, loaded with ammunition, were soon

Stunned sailors view the wreckage at a landing strip on Ford Island.

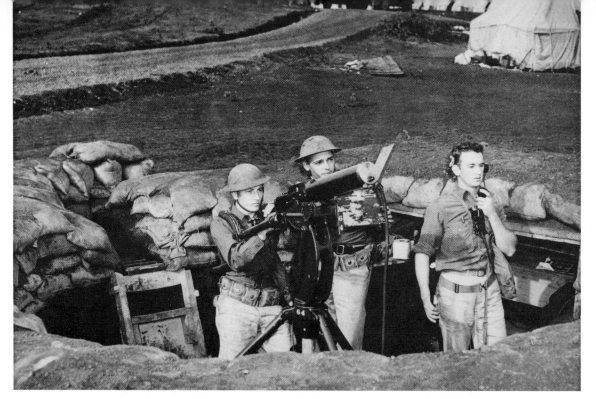

Americans fight back from a machine-gun nest at Wheeler Field.

speeding into the sky to challenge the attackers.
On Battleship Row, antiaircraft fire poured from
the damaged ships. Machine-gun fire rattled even
from the *Arizona*, which had broken in two and
settled into the mud. Below decks, crews on the
damaged ships worked desperately to keep their
ships afloat. If a ship had been hit in the stern
and water was causing her to sink toward the
rear, the sailors flooded the forward
compartments to straighten her out. On the
decks, sailors fought fires, helped the wounded,
and manned antiaircraft guns.

As American sailors battled fires and Japanese
airplanes, they suddenly saw an amazing sight.
The mighty battleship *Nevada*, though damaged

Crewmen fight flames on the beached USS Nevada.

by hits from bombs and torpedoes, was slowly pulling out to sea. As she sailed past the flaming wrecks of her sister ships, the men on the decks cheered. Perhaps the powerful *Nevada* would be able to break out to sea, find the Japanese carriers, and blast them to the bottom.

But as the *Nevada* steamed toward the entrance to the harbor, a second wave of Japanese planes sped toward her. Dive bombers fell from the sky and plunged down toward the moving *Nevada* like hawks seeking prey. In seconds, the brave ship was hit by three bombs, and the commander had to drive her into the beach before she sank and blocked the harbor.

The second wave of Japanese planes attacked the damaged ships of Battleship Row, but this time they were driven away by a barrage of well-aimed antiaircraft fire. Only one Japanese plane managed to get through the barrage to put a bomb into the *Pennsylvania,* but she was in dry dock and could not be sunk.

It was two-thirty in the afternoon on the East Coast. Many Americans were listening to professional football games on their radios, as they did every Sunday afternoon. Midway through a game between the Washington Redskins and the Philadelphia Eagles, the radio broadcast was interrupted to report that Pearl Harbor was under attack. Other radio reports telling of a disaster at Pearl Harbor filtered in.

A crowd gathered outside the White House (below) after radios and newspapers across the nation shouted the news of the surprise attack (right).

Honolulu Star-Bulletin 1st EXTRA

(Associated Press by Transpacific Telephone)

WAR!

SAN FRANCISCO, Dec. 7.—President Roosevelt announced this morning that Japanese planes had attacked Manila and Pearl Harbor.

OAHU BOMBED BY JAPANESE PLANES

SIX KNOWN DEAD, 21 INJURED, AT EMERGENCY HOSPITAL

Attack Made On Island's Defense Areas

Hundreds See City Bombed

Schools Closed

Editorial

When it was all over and the smoke began to clear, the wreckage left behind was incredible.

Some Americans became furious and cursed the Japanese. Others wept, and many prayed. Even today, all Americans old enough to remember December 7, 1941, can recall exactly where they were when they first heard word of the surprise attack on Pearl Harbor.

When the last Japanese plane finally sped back to its carrier, the wreckage of the once powerful Pacific fleet was incredible. Almost all the ships still above water were in flames. The *Oklahoma* floated capsized in the water. The *California* was sunk, and the *Arizona* lay on the bottom of the harbor.

Tony Muncie swam toward Ford Island through water thick with oil. He reached the beach, took two steps, and fell to his hands and knees, panting. The oil soaked his clothes and covered his skin, making him feel twice his weight. He had been lucky—just how lucky he did not yet know. The shock of the first bomb that had hit the *Arizona* had blown him overboard before his ship exploded into a flaming orange ball. Tony lived to fight again, but the ship he was so proud of and his many close friends on the crew remained on the bottom of Pearl Harbor.

At his naval base, thousands of miles from Hawaii, Admiral Yamamoto listened to radio reports from his fleet off Pearl Harbor. The attack had been an overwhelming success. Even he had not expected to crush the United States fleet so completely. Younger officers congratulated him for his victory, but Yamamoto could not share their excitement. He realized that he had won only the first battle in what would be a long war.

Two things troubled Yamamoto. First, there were no American aircraft carriers at Pearl Harbor, so all United States carriers were safe. He believed that in this war, to be fought over vast areas of the Pacific, carriers would become

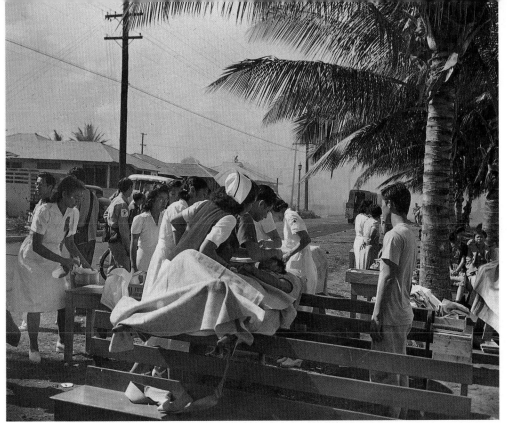

Bombed out of their regular quarters, emergency first-aid workers work outside on the wounded on the morning of the attack.

far more important than battleships. But even more, he was afraid the American people would be so outraged over Japan's surprise attack that they would work together to defeat his country. He wondered what chance tiny Japan would have against a united and angry American people.

Yamamoto went to bed early, telling himself over and over again that this war had not been his idea. He had a very difficult time getting to sleep that night.

At Pearl Harbor, the American forces counted their losses. What had started as a peaceful Sunday morning had become a nightmare. More than twenty-four hundred American sailors, soldiers, and marines were dead. More than

Rescuers had to cut through the hull of the Oklahoma *to reach those trapped inside. More than four hundred men were on the ship when it capsized; only thirty-two were taken out alive.*

eleven hundred had been wounded. Eighteen ships had been lost, and more than three hundred airplanes had been destroyed or badly damaged.

After the last bomb had fallen, American sailors worked desperately to rescue sailors who were trapped inside the capsized *Oklahoma*. From inside watery, pitch-dark compartments, the trapped men banged on walls to guide the rescuers. For days, sailors worked on the decks and underwater, cutting through metal with torches until they could reach their trapped comrades. Only thirty-two men were taken out of the *Oklahoma* alive.

Nineteen-year-old George De Long (below) was one of the few men taken out alive from the USS Oklahoma. *Years later (left), he recalled the experience while touring a ship compartment much like the one he had been trapped in on the* Oklahoma.

The men on the *Arizona*, however, could not be helped. The ship's bottom lay in the mud, and her decks roared with flames. The fire was so hot that no one could get close to her.

On Monday, December 8, President Franklin Delano Roosevelt asked Congress for a declaration of war. In one of the most famous speeches in history, he said: "Yesterday, December 7, 1941—a date that will live in infamy—the United States of America was suddenly and deliberately attacked by naval and air forces of the Empire of Japan . . ." The president's speech was interrupted many times by thundering applause. Even his political

On December 8, President Roosevelt asked Congress to declare war on Japan (left). "Remember Pearl Harbor" became a battle cry of the war and even inspired a popular song (right).

enemies in Congress now wildly cheered the president. All Americans united with Roosevelt and were determined to wage total war.

Pearl Harbor was the worst military defeat in United States history, but out of that defeat came spirit. "Remember Pearl Harbor" became a battle cry heard throughout the war. A popular song was written around the words. Exactly what Admiral Yamamoto had feared had happened. The American people, shocked by Pearl Harbor, would work together toward victory.

26

The sunken USS California *was raised and towed to dry dock.*

Congress granted the president a declaration
of war, and three days later, Germany—an ally of
Japan—declared war on the United States.
America was plunged into the bloodiest war of all
time. The war would end with the dawn of a
nuclear age, when atomic bombs fell on the
Japanese cities of Hiroshima and Nagasaki.

When the smoke cleared at Pearl Harbor,
American engineers worked to salvage the
damaged ships. One by one, the sunken ships
were raised from the water, towed to dry dock,
and repaired. Most of them would fight again.
The *California*, sunk early during the attack
on Pearl Harbor, would be with the United

States fleet that recaptured the Philippines from the Japanese three years later. The brave *Nevada*, which had tried to break out to sea during the attack, would later shell the beaches at Normandy when the United States and her allies invaded Europe.

Five of the seven ships on Battleship Row were repaired, and fought during World War II. The *Oklahoma*, beyond repair, was towed out of the harbor to be sold as scrap metal.

Tony Muncie's ship, the USS *Arizona*, remained on the harbor bottom.

The USS Arizona *on December 10, 1941*

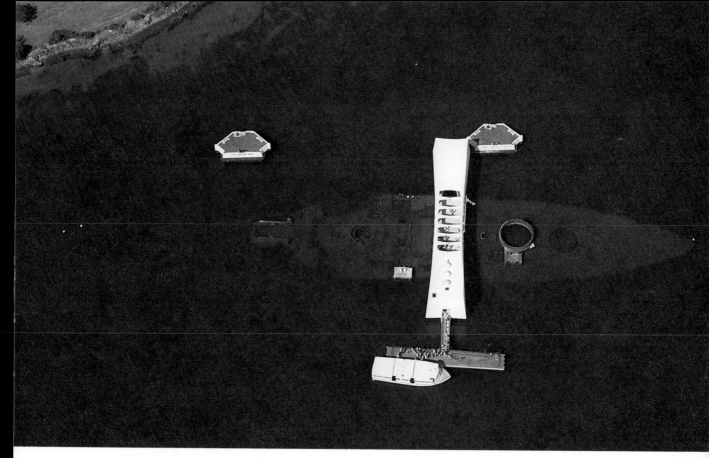

The USS Arizona *Memorial was built directly over the sunken ship.*

On the morning of December 7, 1941, the *Arizona* had a crew of nearly fifteen hundred men. Eleven hundred and seventy-seven of them died on that tragic day. Their ship became their grave, for the bodies of the men were never removed. The navy built a platform with a flagpole over the wreck of the *Arizona*. Every day during World War II, sailors rowed to the platform and raised and lowered the flag in honor of her crew.

The USS *Arizona* Memorial, built over the spot where the *Arizona* lies, was dedicated in 1962. Thousands of tourists visit the shrine every

Visitors at the memorial (above) and a wall at the visitor center showing the names of all who gave their lives at Pearl Harbor (right)

month. Some of them are men who were stationed at Pearl Harbor at the time of the attack. Others served in other World War II battles. Many visitors are children and grandchildren of World War II veterans.

Those who come to pay their respects to the crew of the *Arizona* think of the many men beneath the shrine who died so suddenly and while they were so young.

The USS *Arizona* was stricken from the Naval Vessel Register a year after the attack. But the names of the fallen crew appear inside the memorial. Those who died on that tragic day of December 7, 1941, will never be forgotten.

INDEX

PHOTO CREDITS

Cover, AP/Wide World; 1, © David L. Moore/Dembinsky Photo Assoc.; 2, 3, 4, UPI/Bettmann; 5 (both photos), Official U.S. Navy Photograph; 7, UPI/Bettmann; 8, 9, AP/Wide World; 10, Official U.S. Navy Photograph; 11, 12, 13, 14, 15, 16, AP/Wide World; 17, Official U.S. Navy Photograph; 18, 19, 20 (both photos), 21, AP/Wide World; 23, UPI/Bettmann; 24, AP/Wide World; 25 (top), © David Doubilet; 25 (bottom), George De Long; 26 (left), AP/Wide World; 26 (right), UPI/Bettmann; 27, AP/Wide World; 28, Official U.S. Navy Photograph; 29, © David Doubilet; 30, Photri; 31, © David L. Moore/Dembinsky Photo Assoc.

Picture Identifications
Cover: The sinking of the USS *Arizona*
Page 1: A wall inside the USS *Arizona* Memorial containing the names of the 1,177 servicemen who went down with the ship on December 7, 1941
Page 2: The USS *Arizona* at sea

Project Editor: Shari Joffe
Designer: Karen Yops
Cornerstones of Freedom Logo: David Cunningham

ABOUT THE AUTHOR

R. Conrad Stein was born and raised in Chicago. He enlisted in the U.S. Marine Corps at the age of eighteen and served for three years. He then attended the University of Illinois, where he received a bachelor's degree in history. He later studied in Mexico, earning an advanced degree from the University of Guanajuato.

Mr. Stein is the author of many other books, articles, and short stories for young people. He lives in Chicago with his wife and their daughter Janna.